THE ZION TUNNEL

From Slickrock to Switchback

By Donald T. Garate

The intent of this small volume is to pay tribute to all those who, with insight and perseverence, contributed their individual skills to overcome the seemingly insurmountable obstacle of bringing Zion within the reach of all of us. In so doing, they not only brought many of Zion's wonders within our grasp, but created another wonder in itself at which we can marvel: the Zion-Mt. Carmel Switchbacks and Tunnel.

ACKNOWLEDGMENTS

COVER PHOTO
Visitors look across Pine Creek Canyon from Gallery #1 in the Zion-Mt. Carmel Tunnel.
U.S. DEPARTMENT OF TRANSPORTATION.

TITLE PAGE
The Utah Parks Company, an affiliate of the Union Pacific Railroad, brought the governors, their families, and staffs to the dedication at the tunnel gallery in their tour busses.
ZION NATIONAL PARK COLLECTION.

No historical work can be properly written without the help of those who have a knowledge of the area and circumstances. For this reason the author wishes to express his deepest, heartfelt gratitude to the following people whose kind assistance made the writing of this book possible: Jerome Gifford, J.L. Crawford, Jeff Frank, Lee Wilcox, Bob Wood, Albert Jones, Alma Hirschi, Terry Kratzer, Gene Garate, Jerry Mitchell, Lenard Wilcox, Lloyd Sandberg, George Shamo, Bob Lineback, Christine Dick, Lillian Workman, Fae Winsor, Frances Hepworth, Grant Langston, and Vernon and Velda Wilcox.

The Zion Tunnel—From Slickrock To Switchback— is published by Zion Natural History Association, Inc., a nonprofit organization pledged to aid in the understanding, preservation and interpretation of the scenic and historic features of the Park. The original manuscript has been edited for this publication. If you would like to order a xerox copy of the entire manuscript at $5.00 per copy, or additional copies of this book, please write the Zion Natural History Association, Zion National Park, Springdale, Utah 84767.

Zion National Park Springdale, Utah 84767 800-635-3959 www.zionpark.org
Text and research by Donald T. Garate
Design by Lee Carlman Riddell
Type set in Eurobodoni, Futura and Helvetica
Printed on recycled paper by Paragon Press
ISBN 0-915630-26-5

CONTENTS

Pictured here on the day the final arrangements were made in Washington D.C. for the building of the Zion-Mt. Carmel Highway are Horace M. Albright (left), acting director of the National Park Service, and George H. Dern, Governor of Utah.

PHOTO GIVEN TO ZION NATIONAL PARK SUPERINTENDENT EIVIND T. SCOYEN BY HORACE M. ALBRIGHT.

THE PROBLEM

Historically, Zion National Park, as it is known today, has denied accessibility to ancient Anasazi and Paiute, early pioneer and modern tourist alike. Sheer walls rising as much as 3000 feet above the valley floor deny movement between the canyon and the plateau above. For the ancient Native Americans the problem was one of moving their winter homes from the mild and sunny deserts south of the canyon mouth to the cooler wooded mesas and mountains—their hunting grounds—to the north. Early pioneers faced a similar difficulty in moving their livestock back and forth between the winter range lands below and the summer pastures above the canyon.

Then came the day of the automobile and tourism. Tourists were meant to see Zion, but automobiles were not made for such harsh terrain. Interest was building in the landscape due to the qualities of its scenery, not only at Zion, but throughout southern Utah and northern Arizona. As the nation began to realize the phenomenal beauty of the area, voices began to be heard in Washington demanding that access be made available to Americans everywhere. It would take many years, many dollars and many people to make accessibility of Zion a reality for the common person. When the task was accomplished, three magnificent National Parks—Zion, Bryce and Grand Canyon—would be brought within reach of everyone.

Now three scenic wonders could be seen in one trip, traveling on a modern, paved highway. The connecting route would be only twenty-four miles long, yet it would pass through two tunnels, numerous dynamited road cuts, and a 3.6-mile series of switchbacks stacked on top of themselves in less than a quarter of a square mile. In short, the connection would pierce some of the most rugged, yet magnificent landscape in the world!

LEFT
Because of the ruggedness of Zion, a road from the canyon to the rim was thought to be an impossibility for many years.
PHOTO BY O.M. UHL, DONATED TO ZION NATIONAL PARK BY EVAN S. PICKETT.

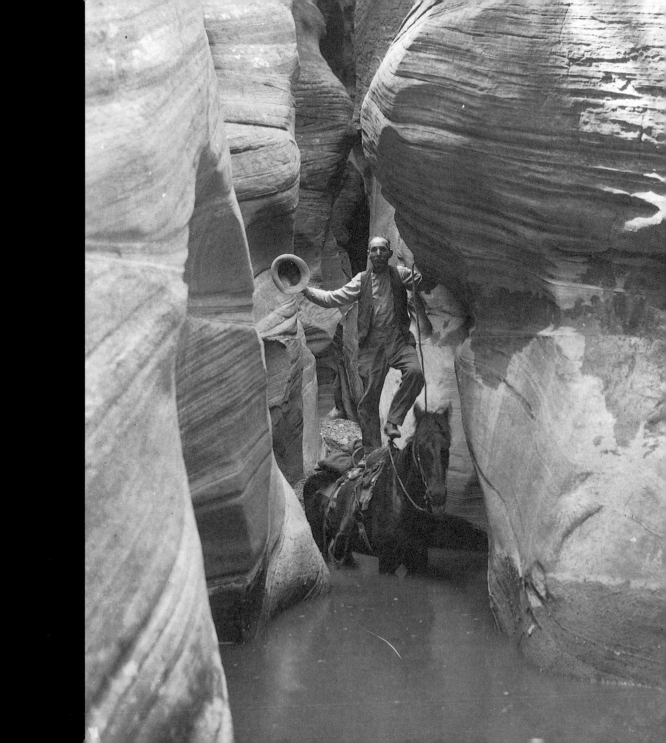

FINDING A SOLUTION

Probably the first and only trail ever built out of Zion Canyon by Native Americans is still partially visible today from the Weeping Rock parking lot. Some twenty steps chiseled into the sheer rock face attest to the fact that the Paiutes, and possibly the Anasazi before them, went out through Echo Canyon to the East Rim. But, oh! It was a precarious trail and pioneer journals record at least one Paiute brave as having fallen and died while descending those steps. And yet, it did provide access, dangerous though it may have been.

Just prior to the turn of the century, following the Paiutes' lead, John Winder, a local stockman raised in Springdale, constructed the first pioneer livestock trail out across the same rock face. This trail, too, was dangerous and tricky. Over the years several cattle and horses were fatally injured in falling from its switchbacks. But only one person was ever seriously injured on it.

When Zion first became a National Monument, the Park Service did extensive work on remodeling Winder's trail and building others. An actual road out of the canyon, however, seemed beyond the reach of everyone. Yet, prior to the 1920s many people began lobbying for just such a road. Finally, in 1923, Howard Means, Chief Engineer of the State of Utah, and B.J. Finch, a district engineer for the Federal Government, were sent to determine, once and for all, if a road could be built out of the canyon.

At first, as with all attempts before them, they met with failure. Then someone introduced them to John Winder. He showed them where the road should go up Pine Creek Canyon. They surveyed the route and determined it was feasible. The only hurdle left was convincing Congress to appropriate money for such an extensive project.

LEFT
The only trail out of Zion Canyon prior to its becoming a National Park was known as the "Big Bend Trail." It was originally used by Native Americans. Later, John Winder, pictured here in the depths of Echo Canyon in 1913, built a trail for driving livestock along the same route. As can be seen from this photograph, it was no thoroughfare.

PHOTO BY J. CECIL ALTER,
E. IRVING ALTER COLLECTION.

RIGHT
After surveying Pine Creek
from the bottom, Finch
and Means went with
Winder out onto the East
Rim to survey down the
canyon from the top. The
pointed peak on the left is
Bridge Mountain. On the
right is the East Temple. It
was between these two
peaks and through this
rugged wilderness that the
new road would be built.
The two engineers went
home fully convinced that,
although expensive, the
project was feasible.

ZION NATIONAL PARK COLLECTION.

A MONUMENTAL TASK
— Work Begins —

By the summer of 1927, building of the Zion-Mt. Carmel Highway was ready to begin. Area promoters, prominent politicians, and the United States Park Service under the capable direction of Stephen T. Mather had convinced a reluctant Congress that the project would work. Money was there, and the contract was let on September 8th of that year to Nevada Contracting Company of Fallon, Nevada.

The project was divided into four sections. Section #1 was the 3.6 miles of switchbacks between the Virgin River and the west entrance to the tunnel. Section #2 was the tunnel itself, and Section #3 was the stretch of road from the east tunnel entrance to the Park boundary. Section #4 was outside the Park and would largely be paid for by the State of Utah. The contract for that section of the road went to Raleigh-Lang Construction Company of Springville, Utah.

The first six men hired by Nevada Contracting Company started work on clearing the road right-of-way up Pine Creek Canyon on September 27, 1927. Under the leadership of the company's superintendent, Stanley Bray, the number of men would swell from six to over 200 in the next couple of years. And, subcontractors and other companies working on the project would hire many more than that.

As men were brought onto the job, they were divided into two crews: one was a road crew building the switchbacks, and the other was a mining crew to build the tunnel. Locals were hired for most of the jobs with the exception of the crew bosses for the tunnel construction. These were a group of sixteen hard rock miners, brought onto the job from all over the United States and Canada, who oversaw the local men hired as tunnel workers and were under the direction of Tunnel Boss Richard N. Scott.

LEFT
Tunnel Boss Dick Scott (right) was part of the original crew of hard rock miners and their families who were brought onto the job to oversee the tunnel construction.

LILLIAN WORKMAN COLLECTION.

Some of the earliest work done on the highway is seen here in lower Pine Creek Canyon from a point near the west end of the plateau where the Contractor's Camp was located. In the extreme lower right corner is an automobile parked in front of a warehouse. An aerial cable tramway ran from just above the warehouse 1200 feet across the canyon to about where the photographer stood to take the picture. Near the center of the picture on the left side of the creek bed is another warehouse. Just beyond it and barely visible are two houses that were occupied by the George and John Shea families. Shea & Shea was the subcontractor that built the rock retaining walls on the switchbacks, one of which can be seen in the left center of the photograph.

PHOTO BY O.M. UHL, DONATED TO ZION
NATIONAL PARK BY EVAN S. PICKETT.

RIGHT
A trail was built from the Contractor's Camp to the face of the cliff to provide access for the tunnel crews. In this picture the camp is still under construction but the trail is visible, running from it across the center of the photograph. In time the trail, surveyed for the company by John Winder, ran from the camp all the way around the face of the cliff to Gallery #4. All materials for building the pilot tunnel as far as the fourth gallery went up this "Pioneer Trail," either carried by the men themselves or transported by horse and cart. Eventually this section of the trail was obliterated by the road crews building the Nevada Switchback. In fact, the enormous boulder just to the right of the sheer cliff face had to be dynamited to prevent it from tumbling down onto the road in one piece.

NEBRASKA STATE HISTORICAL SOCIETY.

THE CONTRACTOR'S CAMP

The first project that had to be completed was the building of a camp to house the many workers that would flood onto the job. The site that was chosen was a flat place on the talus slope just west of what would be called the Nevada Switchback. Since this area was basically inaccessible prior to construction of the road, an aerial tramway had to be erected to carry supplies to the proposed site. This consisted of 1200 feet of one-inch cable that made a 400-foot vertical lift from Pine Creek to the campsite.

Once the tramway was in place in late November, it took the workers just over two weeks to construct the camp which consisted of sixteen "boxcar-type" bunkhouses, 12 cabins, a blacksmith shop and a garage for truck maintenance and repair. The workers that moved in on December 9, 1927, already numbered over a hundred men.

The camp was soon the hub of activity for the project. Workers came and went at all hours of the day and night. Sleep for weary men was difficult. There was the cold in the winter, the heat in the summer, and the constant noise and dust. Night workers in the tunnel carried their cots to the face of the cliff near the tunnel entrance to sleep in the shade during the heat of the day.

Dining at the cook shack was a unique experience. Hungry men would be ravenously eating when the roar of a dynamite explosion would be heard. Everyone would drop their utensils, and run and stand next to the walls. When a few moments had elapsed, they would go back to eating as if nothing had happened. This routine had started following a blast one day when a ten-pound chunk of sandstone came crashing through the roof, landing in the middle of the tables where the men were seated!

LEFT
The aerial tramway cable can be seen as a black line in the upper right of the picture. The white line is a cable that ran from it down to the ground and was used for hoisting the platform loaded with supplies up to the level of the main cable. The upper bulkhead can be seen across the canyon as a tiny white triangle in the upper left ¼ of the picture. The buildings stored dynamite and other materials.
J.L. CRAWFORD COLLECTION

AN ENGINEERING MARVEL
— Driving The Pilot Tunnel —

It was decided that the most economical and quickest way to bore the tunnel would be to first drill a small shaft or pilot tunnel. When this was accomplished, another crew would follow and "ring drill" the pilot bore and blast it out to a full twenty-two feet wide and sixteen feet high. Since ventilation would be a problem in a tunnel slightly over a mile long, five windows, or galleries, were planned and the tunnel would be no more than forty feet inside the cliff face. Just before construction began, engineers decided to build a sixth gallery (see map pages 26-27).

A "Pioneer Trail" was built along the face of the cliff to provide access to these galleries. Work on the tunnel began in early November at Galleries #1 and #6. When these galleries were into the mountain the desired depth, crews began drilling both directions from both galleries around the clock.

When the connection between Galleries #1 and #6 was made, work had already begun on Gallery #2. When the pilot bore was blasted out of the mountain at the west entrance, crews were drifting both directions from #2, and work had commenced at #3 where a 235-foot tramway had been built to carry materials and equipment from the Pioneer Trail to the cliff face.

When the Pioneer Trail reached the site of Gallery #4, it was found that the gallery would be 200 feet above. So, rather than try to build scaffolding up the outside of the wall, a nearly vertical shaft, or stope, was drilled to the level of the tunnel floor, and the fourth gallery was blasted out from inside the mountain.

When the last connection was made between Galleries #3 and #4, the crews began drifting east from #4. When they reached the point for Gallery #5, they again blasted it out from the inside of the mountain at a point along Pine Creek where the canyon walls are about twenty feet apart, and yet, from the level of the tunnel it is several hundred feet to the canyon floor.

After completing the fifth gallery, the workers continued drifting east until the pilot bore broke out of the mountain on the side of a cliff above Pine Creek.

LEFT
The first dynamite blast in construction of the tunnel took place on November 8, 1927 at the site of Gallery #1, the largest gallery in the tunnel. Drilling the hole for this charge was accomplished atop a 45-foot scaffold, using regular jackhammers. Once the gallery was into the mountain the proper depth, work on a pilot shaft (8'x 9') began running in both directions. Drilling for the pilot shaft was done with "water liner" drills to keep dust from building up inside the shaft. Water for these drills was piped to the tunnel face from Pine Creek, 500 vertical feet below.

U.S. DEPARTMENT OF TRANSPORTATION.

TOP RIGHT
Gallery #1, shown under construction, is 100 feet long and is located 45 feet up the cliff face.

U.S. DEPARTMENT OF TRANSPORTATION, NEBRASKA STATE HISTORICAL SOCIETY.

BOTTOM RIGHT
Workmen begin opening up Gallery #6. Originally, only five galleries were planned for the tunnel, numbered consecutively running east from #1. However, the engineers decided to build a sixth gallery for better ventilation and lighting between the first gallery and the west entrance to the tunnel. Work was started on this gallery just one week after drilling began on Gallery #1. However, the first gallery was already 30 feet into the cliff face at that time.

NEBRASKA STATE HISTORICAL SOCIETY.

LEFT
This view of Gallery #6 is from the Pioneer Trail, which was only wide enough for a horse and small cart. Note the 5-inch compressed air line which eventually ran nearly a mile from the compressor plant to the 200-foot stope near Gallery #4.

NEBRASKA STATE HISTORICAL SOCIETY.

TOP RIGHT
Shift Boss Joe Halverstead is operating one of several Sullivan Air Tuggers that were used for hauling material and equipment to the galleries and also for dragging the mining cars to the galleries for unloading rubble from the pilot tunnel. A compressed air line can be seen running to the tugger.

LILLIAN WORKMAN COLLECTION.

BOTTOM RIGHT
Workers begin construction of the pilot shaft. Note the engineer's transit between the two workers in the background. Before each shift an engineer would determine centerline and direction for the drillers.

NEBRASKA STATE HISTORICAL SOCIETY.

LEFT
This view looks west from Gallery #6 in the pilot tunnel. Note the air and water lines to the left of the tracks. The shaft was lighted by electric lights and ventilated by electric fans after the dynamite blasts. Power was brought onto the site in January, 1928. Prior to that all work was accomplished by carbide lights and dynamite fumes were blown away with compressed air.

U.S. DEPARTMENT OF TRANSPORTATION.

 RIGHT
This view of the construction of Gallery #3 shows the 235-foot tramway, and a powder and tool shed. A skip hauling materials to the tunnel is about a third of the way up the tramway.

U.S. DEPARTMENT OF TRANSPORTATION.

LEFT

The builders of the Pioneer Trail ran into a major obstacle just before reaching Gallery #4. The trail had to be blasted into a rounding cliff face some 80 feet above the canyon floor. It was steep, narrow and treacherous and the flat place it reached was still nearly 200 feet below the site of the proposed gallery. This prompted the Contractor to request a variance to build a vertical shaft up the inside of the cliff to the floor of the tunnel (see map on pages 26-27).

J.L. CRAWFORD COLLECTION.

RIGHT

The opening of the vertical shaft, or stope, is located 200 feet below and about 100 feet west around the cliff face from Gallery #4. The men are seated in front of the tool and powder shed, where they often came to eat their lunches while the rounds were being shot off up inside the tunnel.

LILLIAN WORKMAN COLLECTION.

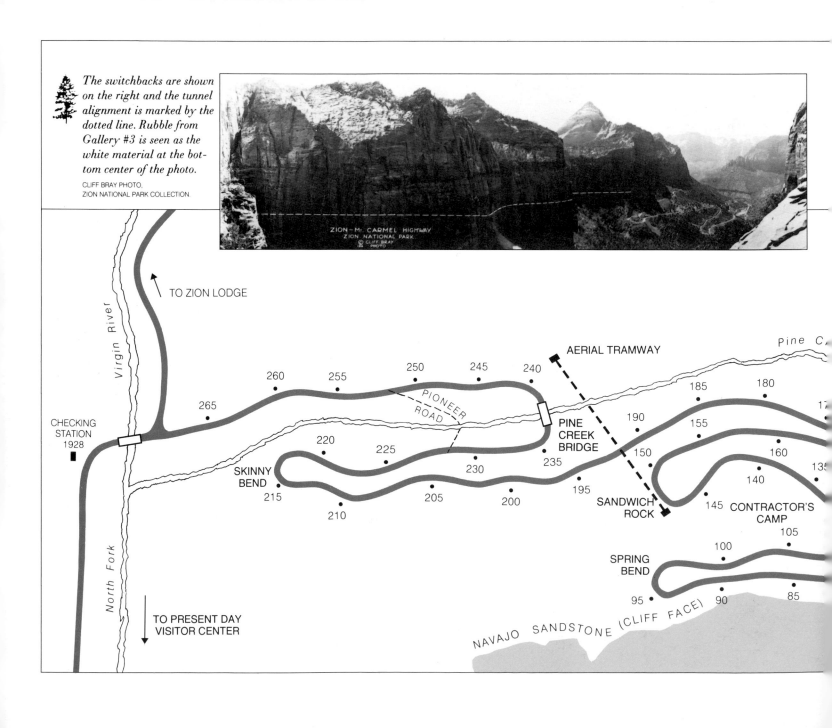

The switchbacks are shown on the right and the tunnel alignment is marked by the dotted line. Rubble from Gallery #3 is seen as the white material at the bottom center of the photo.

CLIFF BRAY PHOTO,
ZION NATIONAL PARK COLLECTION.

ZION – Mt. CARMEL HIGHWAY
ZION NATIONAL PARK
© CLIFF BRAY
PHOTO

Virgin River

TO ZION LODGE

CHECKING
STATION
1928

North Fork

TO PRESENT DAY
VISITOR CENTER

PIONEER ROAD

260   255   250   245   240

265

220   225
SKINNY
BEND   230
215   205   200   235

210

AERIAL TRAMWAY

Pine C

185   180

190   155

150   160

195   140   135

SANDWICH
ROCK

145   CONTRACTOR'S
CAMP

105

PINE
CREEK
BRIDGE

SPRING
BEND   100

95   90   85

NAVAJO SANDSTONE (CLIFF FACE)

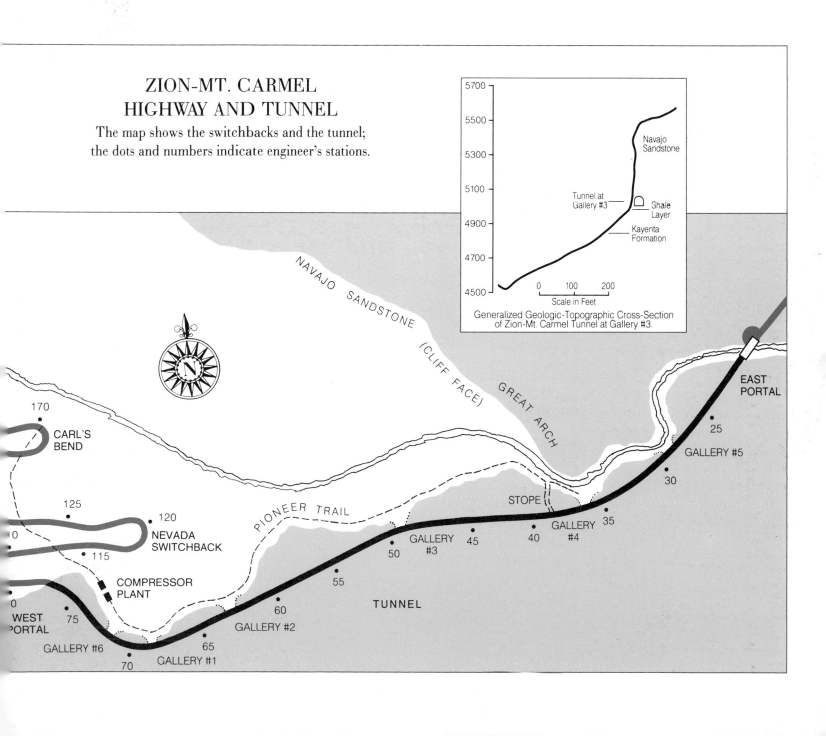

ZION-MT. CARMEL
HIGHWAY AND TUNNEL

The map shows the switchbacks and the tunnel;
the dots and numbers indicate engineer's stations.

NAVAJO SANDSTONE (CLIFF FACE)

GREAT ARCH

**Generalized Geologic-Topographic Cross-Section
of Zion-Mt. Carmel Tunnel at Gallery #3.**

Navajo Sandstone

Tunnel at Gallery #3

Shale Layer

Kayenta Formation

Scale in Feet

0   100   200

EAST PORTAL

170

CARL'S BEND

25

GALLERY #5

30

125

120

NEVADA SWITCHBACK

115

STOPE

35

GALLERY #4

40

45

GALLERY #3

50

COMPRESSOR PLANT

55

PIONEER TRAIL

60

TUNNEL

WEST PORTAL

75

GALLERY #2

65

GALLERY #6

70

GALLERY #1

THE SWITCHBACKS

As work was progressing in the pilot shaft, crews were pushing the road up the steep side of the talus slope toward a point the engineers had marked for the tunnel's West Portal. Both the tunnel crew and the road crew hoped to be the first to arrive at the site. A spirit of competition intensified daily as each crew neared the ultimate destination. A rough preliminary road arrived at the site on February 9, 1928. Four days later the miners blasted out of the mountain at the same point.

The road crew's equipment consisted of one P&H 1¾-yard power shovel, two ¾-yard shovels, a fleet of several chain driven "bulldog" Mack dump trucks and lots of dynamite. As the road progressed up the mountain, each of the switchbacks was given a name; "Skinny Bend" describing the first; "Carl's Bend" for Carl Bergdahl, a job supervisor; "Sandwich Rock" for a huge boulder of like appearance; "Nevada Switchback" for the contractor; and "Spring Bend" for the spring from which water was piped to the Contractor's Camp.

Much difficulty was encountered at the Nevada Switchback. The mountainside kept sluffing away as the road progressed, leaving an unsightly scar. This particular point on the road was by far the worst, but the entire 3.6 miles was subject to rock slides. Retaining walls had to be built along much of the road to hold it on the side of the mountain.

It was a rock slide on the switchbacks that caused one of the two fatal casualties during the nearly three years the route was under construction. An enormous sandstone boulder pinned Mac McClain against the tracks of one of the power shovels. The other death occurred in the pilot tunnel on the night of July 1, 1928, when the connection was made between Galleries #3 and #4. Johnny Morrison, a crew boss and hard rock miner from Canada, lost his life from inhaling too much sand and dynamite fumes.

LEFT
Rock was quarried from the Springdale Member of the Moenave for use in the retaining walls.
ZION NATIONAL PARK COLLECTION.

TOP LEFT
Early road work is being done on the switchbacks.

NEBRASKA STATE HISTORICAL SOCIETY.

TOP RIGHT
One of the P&H ¾-yard power shovels and two of the "bulldog" Mack dump trucks are shown constructing the first switchback above the Pine Creek Bridge.

U.S. DEPARTMENT OF TRANSPORTATION, NEBRASKA STATE HISTORICAL SOCIETY.

BOTTOM LEFT
This view of the Nevada Switchback (foreground) and Spring Bend (in the distance) was taken from the East Temple. The tremendous slide caused by the road construction at the Nevada Switchback is plainly shown.

ANDERSON PHOTO, ZION NATIONAL PARK COLLECTION.

RIGHT
The tunnel mouth (right) and the switchbacks have been connected. Also shown from left to right are Galleries #2 and #1.

LYNNE CLARK OLD PHOTO COLLECTION DONATED BY HIRSCHI & S. RUESCH FAMILY ORGANIZATION.

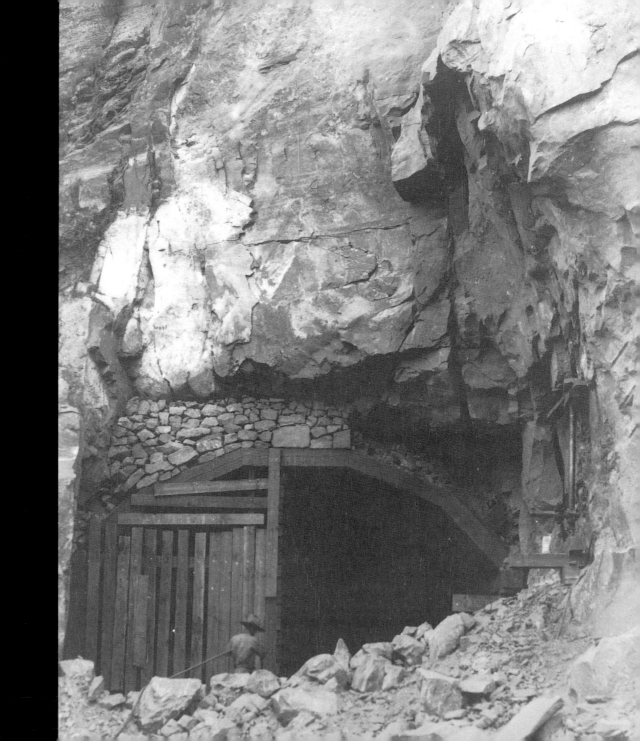

DRIVING THE FULL BORE

Five days after the pilot tunnel reached the west entrance on February 13, 1928, separate crews began "ring drilling" to expand the shaft to its full size. For this operation a drill was placed on a heavy iron spindle in the middle of the floor of the pilot shaft. One hole was drilled straight up into the ceiling. Then the drill was rotated and a series of holes was drilled from that point down to the floor on each side. When the seventeen holes constituting the "ring" were complete, the drill was moved down the tunnel three feet and another series of holes drilled. When twelve of these rings were complete, a blasting crew would load and touch them off, blasting out 36 feet of full bore tunnel.

The enormous rubble pile would then be cleared away. Unlike the pilot shaft in which the debris was hauled in mining cars and dumped out the galleries, the contractor's Mack trucks backed into the full bore shaft and hauled the blasted material down onto the switchbacks, dumping it wherever fill was needed. For loading the trucks inside the tunnel, the contractor brought an Erie Power Shovel onto the job. This compact piece of equipment operated on compressed air to cut down on the amount of exhaust fumes inside the shaft.

This was a mechanized operation that did not require the numbers of men that the pilot tunneling did. Work progressed rapidly, and although the ring drillers had started three months later than the pilot crew, they would only be one month behind them when they blasted out of the mountain on the east side.

Dynamite blasts could be heard daily coming from the switchbacks. The noise of explosions was also heard in succession at each of the galleries as blasting occurred inside the tunnel. This, coupled with the echoes made by each detonation, kept Pine Creek Canyon in constant reverberation.

LEFT
The West Portal was shored up at the beginning of the full bore drilling.
KITTREDGE PHOTO,
ZION NATIONAL PARK COLLECTION.

TOP RIGHT
This shows the working
face of the full bore tunnel-
ing operation. The pilot
tunnel is beyond the
timbered rubble pile.

BOTTOM LEFT
Ring drilling with this type
of drill in the pilot tunnel
averaged one foot per
minute in the sandstone
of the tunnel.

BOTTOM RIGHT
The Erie Air Shovel
excavated the full bore.
One of the Mack dump
trucks is backed in for
loading; note the rock
caught between its dual
tires on the right. Origi-
nally the trucks had hard
rubber tires but they were
constantly getting stuck in
the sand created by the
dynamite blasts in the
tunnel. This caused the
Contractor to have to buy
the new pneumatic tires
shown here and outfit all
the trucks with them.

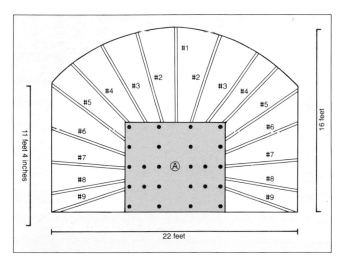

TOP LEFT

Shaded area - Pilot Tunnel
Black dots - represent
position and number of
holes drilled in pilot bore.
Top row of holes - Back holes
Second row - Breast holes
Third row - Cut holes
Fourth row - Relievers (easers)
Fifth row - Lifters
Ⓐ *- is the position of the*
spindle on which the stoper
drill revolved for "ring
drilling" the full bore
tunnel.
Unshaded area - ground
taken out between the pilot
and full bore sections
Double lines - with
numbers indicate ring drill
holes and their positions.

TOP RIGHT
The full bore is in progress
at the site of Gallery #1.

BOTTOM
The timbered west section
of the Zion Tunnel as it
looked during the driving
of the full bore.

COMPLETION OF A MONUMENTAL TASK

On Sunday, September 16, 1928, the pilot crew holed through at the east entrance. It had taken 313 days to get to that point. At that time the ring drillers were already east of the fifth gallery, and the Erie Air Shovel was working right at the gallery itself. The ring drilling was completed to the entrance on October 19th. The following day at 6:00 p.m. the little air shovel completed cleaning the shaft. It had taken eleven months and twelve days to blast the tunnel through the mountain. Now the only thing left to do was blast the uneven places, or "shoot the tights," as the miners said.

As soon as a temporary bridge was built across Pine Creek at the east entrance, power shovels and dump trucks were moved out through the tunnel. Work was begun building the road toward the Park's east boundary to meet the Raleigh-Lang Company whose workers were nearing the boundary from the west. Much blasting had to be done to make cuts in the slickrock country on the east. A short road tunnel and four water tunnels to carry water under the road were built. Many rock culverts and retaining walls also had to be created.

The Reynolds-Ely Construction Company of Springville contracted to build the bridges on the route and Ora Bundy Construction of Ogden did all the curbs, paving and other finish work.

By the end of 1929 the road was nearly completed. In fact, a car could be driven over the entire route, but it was not yet open to the public. That would not come until the formal dedication on July 4th, 1930. Even then, the finishing touches on the Pine Creek Bridge were not completed. The contractor's foreman had made the bridge such a work of art that he missed the completion deadline by six days. The last rock work was finished on July 10, 1930.

LEFT
Early visitors enjoy
the view from the
West Portal.

PHOTO BY O.M. UHL, DONATED TO ZION NATIONAL PARK BY EVAN S. PICKETT.

 TOP LEFT
Construction of this deep cut just east of the tunnel was the option chosen rather than building another tunnel at that site.
U.S. DEPARTMENT OF TRANSPORTATION.

 TOP CENTER
This framework was constructed in preparation to build the permanent reinforced concrete bridge at the East Portal.
PHOTO BY O.M. UHL, DONATED TO ZION NATIONAL PARK BY EVAN S. PICKETT.

BOTTOM LEFT
Paving the tunnel was often a tight fit.
U.S. DEPARTMENT OF TRANSPORTATION.

LEFT
The newly-completed bridge on upper Pine Creek is seen from the East Portal.
STANDARD OIL COMPANY PHOTO, ZION NATIONAL PARK COLLECTION

TOP LEFT
*A road crew is building
a sandstone arch culvert
east of the tunnel before
the roadway was blasted
through the ridge to
the left.*

PHOTO BY O.M. UHL, DONATED TO ZION
NATIONAL PARK BY EVAN S. PICKETT.

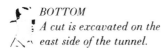 *TOP CENTER*
*Water tunnels were
constructed on the east side
of the tunnel for diverting
water away from the road.*

U.S. DEPARTMENT OF TRANSPORTATION.

 BOTTOM
*A cut is excavated on the
east side of the tunnel.*

JEROME GIFFORD COLLECTION,
DONATED BY VELLA WILLARD PAOLASSO.

RIGHT
*Workers are constructing
a rock retaining wall east
of the tunnel.*

PARKER PHOTO,
ZION NATIONAL PARK COLLECTION.

THE DEDICATION

It was originally intended to dedicate the Zion-Mt. Carmel Highway and Tunnel in June of 1930. However, the governors of the 48 states were scheduled to be in conference in Salt Lake City from June 30 to July 2. It was planned to take the governors on a tour of Zion, Bryce and the Grand Canyon anyway, so it was decided to hold the dedication in conjunction with the conference. And, what could be a better day than Independence Day? So, the formal dedication was set for July 4th, 1930.

The dignitaries arrived in Zion on the afternoon of July 3rd and spent the night at Zion Lodge. There were both afternoon and evening programs at the lodge, and the following morning everyone gathered at Gallery #1 in the tunnel where a speaker's stand and chairs were waiting. Bunting and United States flags adorned the gallery and the tunnel entrance. In all, there were over a thousand people who attended the dedication.

Eivind T. Scoyen, Zion's first superintendent, acted as host. An all male choir from St. George sang various patriotic and pioneer songs during the ceremony. Heber J. Grant, president of the Church of Jesus Christ of Latter-day Saints offered the invocation. Horace M. Albright, Director of the National Park Service, was introduced as master of ceremonies. Speakers included Thomas H. MacDonald, Chief of the United States Bureau of Public Roads, and B.J. Finch, District Engineer, who formally presented the road to Mr. Albright and the National Park Service. After several dignitaries of the various road commissions were introduced, Utah's Governor George H. Dern was the concluding speaker.

The party broke up, and the governors loaded into Union Pacific busses to complete their tour. The group of dignitaries and several hundred other people who had attended the dedication continued on along the new route to Mt. Carmel Junction, officially opening the Zion-Mt. Carmel Highway for public use.

LEFT
Dedication ceremonies were held at Gallery #1 on July 4, 1930.
ZION NATIONAL PARK COLLECTION.

EPILOGUE

Today the tunnel is basically the same as it was upon its completion over sixty years ago. However, because of the softness of the sandstone through which it passes, much reinforcing has been done and concrete ribs now give added support to the tunnel's entire length. Collapse of a sandstone pillar west of Gallery #3 in 1958 broke the top out of that gallery and flushed tons of debris back into the tunnel, causing its closure for several weeks. Because of that collapse, the tunnel is now monitored electronically twenty-four hours a day to warn of such a thing happening while cars are present.

The switchbacks are also basically the same as the day they were completed, although much maintenance is required to keep them from slipping off the side of the mountain.

Due to an immense increase in the volume of traffic and in the size of vehicles passing through the tunnel, visitors can no longer pull off at the galleries to enjoy the magnificent views there. In recent years large vehicles, including tour buses, motorhomes and trailers, were involved in more and more accidents and near misses in the tunnel. A study by the Federal Highway Administration in early 1989 found that large vehicles could not negotiate the curves of the tunnel without crossing the center line. To ensure safety, the National Park Service began an escort service in the spring of that year. Rangers posted at either end of the tunnel during the busy season convert tunnel traffic to one-way for larger vehicles. This service, for which a special fee is charged, was provided for almost 23,000 large vehicles in fiscal year 1990. In the slower season, drivers of large vehicles make advance arrangements for an escort.

At this time, studies are in progress by the National Park Service and Federal Highway Administration to determine the feasibility of widening the existing tunnel or drilling a parallel tunnel deeper in the cliff to allow for one-way traffic in both tunnels. For the present, the existing tunnel remains a wonder to be admired.

LEFT
A busload of visitors poses for this group photograph at Gallery #1.
ZION NATIONAL PARK COLLECTION.

51

REFERENCES

Riders explore the East Rim Trail—orginally called "Big Bend Trail" or "John's Back Door"— on September 11, 1929. This photograph was taken just west of the narrows where John Winder was pictured in 1913 (page 6).

PHOTO BY GEORGE GRANT, ZION NATIONAL PARK COLLECTION.

Crawford, J.L. Taped interview with Donald T. Garate, St. George, Utah, December 10, 1987.

Dern, George H. Talk given at the dedication of the Zion-Mt. Carmel Highway, July 4, 1930.

Finch, B.J. Talk given at the dedication of the Zion-Mt. Carmel Highway, July 4, 1930.

Freeman, Lewis R. "The Hanging Highway of Zion." *Travel Magazine*, Robert M. McBride and Company, NY, June 1930.

Gifford, Jerome. Taped interview with Donald T. Garate, Springdale, Utah, December 3, 1987.

Hirschi, Alma. Taped interview with Donald T. Garate, Virgin, Utah, December 7, 1987.

Iron County Record. "Tunnel Will Link Mountain Highways." Charles H. Bigelow, Cedar City, Utah, July 27, 1928.

Jones, Albert. Taped interview with Donald T. Garate, Virgin, Utah, December 7,1987.

Langston, Grant. Taped interview with Donald T. Garate, Hurricane, Utah, January 4, 1988.

Mahan, Russel and Mamie. Taped interview with J.L. Crawford, St. George, Utah, June 14, 1979.

Means, Howard C. Autobiography typescript. Utah State Historical Society, Salt Lake City, Utah, 1947-48.

Report on Inspection and Rehabilitation Recommen-dations—Gallery #3. Zion-Mt. Carmel Tunnel, Zion National Park, Utah, National Park Service, September 1978.

Salt Lake Tribune. Assorted articles, Salt Lake City, Utah, 1923-30.

Scoyen, Eivind T. Taped interview with Lucy C. Schiefer and Jerome Gifford, Springdale, Utah, 1971.

Shamo, George. Taped interview with Donald T. Garate, Hurricane, Utah, December 20, 1987 and January 2, 1988.

Stability Evaluation and Design Recommendations Zion-Mt. Carmel Tunnel, Zion National Park, U.S. Department of the Interior, National Park Service, June 1980.

Stroud, Tully. "The Bryce Canyon Auto and Hiking Guide." Paragon Press, Salt Lake City, Utah, 1983.

U.S. Department of Agriculture, Bureau of Public Roads, Survey, Engineer, Completion and Final Inspection Reports, Denver, Colorado, 1927-1930.

Washington County News. Assorted articles, St. George, Utah, 1927-30.

Wilcox, Lee. Interview with Donald T. Garate, Virgin, Utah, February 29, 1988.

Wilcox, Lenard. Interview with Donald T. Garate, Virgin, Utah, February 29, 1988.

Wilcox, Vernon. Taped interview with Donald T. Garate, Virgin, Utah, February 21, 1988.

Winder, Dan. Taped interview with J.L. Crawford, Springdale, Utah, July 1975.

Woodbury, Angus M. "A History of Southern Utah and Its National Parks." Utah State Historical Society, Salt Lake City, Utah, 1944.

Workman, Lillian. Taped interview with Donald T. Garate, Hurricane, Utah, January 2, 1988.

Zion National Park, Superintendents Monthly Reports, 1927-1930.